At David C Cook, we equip the local church around
the corner and around the globe to make disciples.
Come see how we are working together—go to
**www.davidccook.org**. Thank you!

*transforming lives together*

# TOGETHER

*a journal for mom & me*

# TOGETHER
*a journal for mom & me*

A Guided Experience
Connecting Moms and Kids
to God and Each Other

*Kara-Kae James*

DAVID C COOK

*transforming lives together*

TOGETHER, A JOURNAL FOR MOM AND ME
Published by David C Cook
4050 Lee Vance Drive
Colorado Springs, CO 80918 U.S.A.

Integrity Music Limited, a Division of David C Cook
Brighton, East Sussex BN1 2RE, England

The graphic circle C logo is a registered trademark of David C Cook.

The website addresses recommended throughout this book are offered as a resource to you. These websites are not intended in any way to be or imply an endorsement on the part of David C Cook, nor do we vouch for their content.

Unless otherwise noted, all Scripture quotations are taken from the Christian Standard Bible®, Copyright © 2017 by Holman Bible Publishers. Used by permission. Christian Standard Bible® and CSB® are federally registered trademarks of Holman Bible Publishers. Scripture quotations marked THE MESSAGE are taken from THE MESSAGE. Copyright © by Eugene H. Peterson 1993, 2002. Used by permission of Tyndale House Publishers, Inc.; NIV are taken from THE HOLY BIBLE, NEW INTERNATIONAL VERSION®, NIV® Copyright © 1973, 1978, 1984, 2011 by Biblica, Inc.® Used by permission. All rights reserved worldwide; and NLT are taken from the *Holy Bible*, New Living Translation, copyright © 1996, 2007 by Tyndale House Foundation. Used by permission of Tyndale House Publishers, Inc., Carol Stream, Illinois 60188. All rights reserved.

ISBN 978-0-8307-7312-1

© 2020 Kara-Kae James
The Author is represented by Alive Literary Agency, 7680 Goddard Street, Suite 200, Colorado Springs, CO 80920, www.aliveliterary.com.

The Team: Alice Crider, Laura Derico, Jack Campbell, Susan Murdock
Cover Design: Jon Middel
Cover Photo: Getty Images

Printed in the United States of America
First Edition 2020

1 2 3 4 5 6 7 8 9 10

121619

*For Jessi, Zoey, and Kenzi.*

*You were the inspiration for this journal, and it's always been one of my greatest joys to learn with you, grow with you, and just be together! What a joy and a privilege to be your mom.*

# Contents

## Dear Mom,

It's so easy for us to walk into parenting knowing exactly what we think we will and will not do. We typically take our own experiences and create in our minds the perfect-parent scenario, and that's exactly what we set out to achieve. Then we actually begin raising children and realize every child is completely different and nothing like what we expected. Even if a child is a "textbook" case of a healthy child, there's always something along the way that throws us and takes us back to step one: having no idea what we're doing.

You wear many hats as a parent, and in each stage of parenting a different hat comes into play. When your children are young, you are the caretaker. This exhausting, physically draining stage is filled with constant diapers, sippy-cup refills, Cheerios on the floor, and crayon masterpieces on your walls. It's a beautiful and trying time. Then one day that wall-drawing, Cheerio-spilling tiny person wakes up and you realize you have a fourth grader with an attitude and a mind of her own. Suddenly you're wishing for the days of scrubbing crayon off the walls, wiping dirty faces, and kissing scraped knees.

This is such an important season as you put on a new hat and your child ventures into the world of long division, friendships, hurt feelings, big emotions, and—dare we say it—the opposite sex. (Bring back the Cheerios, right?) As you step out of the season of doing it all and become a little more hands-off, you don't want to lose your child. You want to stay connected to him emotionally so he knows you are a safe space, a place to come to talk through the hard times, celebrate the good times, and grow together through it all.

You may be refusing to admit what stage comes next. Many times, children enter their teen years and build up walls against their parents. It's a basic human instinct to turn away from our caretakers and want to venture out on our own. During the years before your kids become teenagers, building trust and an environment for open communication is incredibly valuable. Instead of approaching your child's teen years with fingers crossed that it will go well, why not take intentional steps early on to open doors to a better future?

My dream for this book is that you would experience deeper connection with God, with yourself, and with your child. This is more than just a journal; this is a journey. A journey takes time; it takes work. Put in the work and you will see beautiful rewards!

# How to Use This Journal

This journal is a tool to help build an unshakable foundation so you can enter the teen years together without fear or barriers. While it is geared for ages 8–12, you could use the practices cultivated here well into those teen years! We want to see communication and trust become a healthy foundation on which every mom can build a relationship with her child.

Openness with your children is so important, and learning some foundational aspects of how to communicate will help us all be more open and loving toward one another. Let's look at a few key components of communication to think about working on as we open this book.

*Create spaces of open communication.* Think about times you've had some really great conversations with your kids. We often think we can only have really meaningful conversations if we are sitting face to face, with no distractions, but sometimes that can make a child close down instead of open up. Creating open and fluid conversation in daily routines can help make you and your children feel comfortable talking together in your everyday space.

*Be relatable.* Your kids want to know that you are a human being, just like them. If they see you as a stark authority figure with no backstory, they won't see the point in sharing their own stories. Relate with them and share with them as you feel appropriate. Letting your kids see that you are a person with a story will help build trust in your relationship.

*Ask specific questions.* Help children build their stories. When they come home from school telling you about X, Y, and Z, ask questions about A, B, and C. This not only shows your interest in their story, but helps them grow emotionally, improve their communication skills, and better understand the story they are telling. Learning to be storytellers in whatever capacity fits their personality helps them become more open communicators. Asking specific questions also shows your interest in their story and encourages them to take their conversation with you to the next level. You can move beyond the small talk of simply what happened at school that day to really sharing in each other's lives.

*Pay attention to details.* Kids may run for the hills if you start asking them how something made them *feel*, but if you listen well to the details in their stories, you will gain a better understanding of what is really happening inside your children. For example, if your child says, "Math is always terrible," and then goes on to talk about two kids who had a fight during the class, you may want to follow up with, "Are kids like that why math class is terrible for you, or is it just that you are bored?" The child's answer can then lead you into deeper parts of the story. Take time to listen, pay close attention, and ask honest questions about things that make you curious, and you'll avoid sounding like you are grilling your child.

*Remember that your story matters too.* Most of us make the mistake of always asking the basics, "How was school?" and your children fall into always giving the same answers, like robots. Tell your story too, inviting them to ask questions and relate how their own experiences are different from or similar to yours. Share about a hard thing at work that day and see what they follow up with. Tell about a deadline to see what it triggers with them. Think about it: Why would they want to open up to you if you aren't opening up to them?

The world tells us that we can't have a good relationship with our teenagers. We are taught that we are just expected to have hard years with them, but we want to break down those stereotypes. It's our desire to build strong relationships and communication during the early years with our children so by the time they enter the teen years, we've already built a foundation to grow on.

Share in this journal with an open heart and an open mind, and your child will follow. Be creative with your communication, and then step outside this book to build an even deeper foundation. We are praying for your journey as you take steps toward more intimate communication with your children!

---

You will find three main sections in the book, each divided up into categories of their own. Get to know these categories, and then find a pattern that works for you and your child. Maybe you homeschool and can implement this book into your morning routine. Or maybe you are in an extremely busy season of life and can only find time to do it on Saturday afternoons. There's no pressure or expectation here—you do you!

Below you will find a breakdown of each section so you can better understand how to navigate this journey to benefit you and your child.

## JUST FOR US

This is where things get really fun. This is the heart and soul of the book, where we really connect with our kids and spend quality time TOGETHER—because that's what it's all about after all, right? In this section, you will find four categories:

### TALK Together

Fun and creative guided-conversation prompts will help you and your child journal and/or talk back and forth with each other. Stretch your imagination and share exciting stories. Be sure to use the blank pages provided to create your own prompts!

### Have FUN Together

Games, silly questions, and other fun interactive experiences will give you a chance to laugh and play together. This is a place for moms to be kids again and kids to enjoy their moms!

### Go DEEP Together

Write out prayers for each other. Read, interpret, and apply Scripture together. These pages offer a safe space to ask for prayer or help.

### CREATE Together

Get your creative juices flowing! From coloring pages to recipes and more, these creative inspirations will give you opportunities to connect with each other in new and fresh ways.

## JUST FOR KIDS

Freedom for children to explore their faith, read Scripture, journal, and pray for their family can all be found in the Just for Kids section. Sons and daughters of all ages need to know they are important and seen by God and by their moms, and these pages will help them do that. Every kid will also be given the opportunity to face hard situations with Scripture and prayer.

Encourage your child to own her section and spend time in it, but be available to guide as needed. Kids can also use this space to track memories and special things happening in their lives.

## JUST FOR MOMS

For Mom only—find prayer prompts, Scripture, and more in these pages. Reflect on who God made you to be as a mom, and focus on praying for your child. There's also a place to track memories and moments of gratitude to record this special season with your child. Feel free to clip this section out to keep it just for you ... for now. Later, this will be a meaningful keepsake for your child—allowing him to read your words and know how loved he was, and still is!

### Fun Tip

We encourage you to create a "mailbox" space in your home to keep the journal so you can pass it back and forth with your child easily and keep it safe, undamaged by daily life. This journal will be a great keepsake for parents and children to remember the childhood years—together!

# FREQUENTLY ASKED QUESTIONS

*What if I have multiple children?*

If you have more than one child, we recommend going through the journal with one child at a time. An idea for your family could be to choose a specific age (age 10, for example) and go through the journal with your kids when they reach that age. This will give you dedicated time to walk through it with each of them.

You will want to get a journal for each child so they may make it their own and have it as a keepsake. However, while you'll want to use the journal as a tool to connect with one child at a time, you can use some of the activities or craft suggestions to involve other children, if that works for your family.

*Should I use it daily?*

It's really up to you and what fits your schedule. You could plan to use it daily, or during a season. If you have more time in the summer when your kids are out of school, maybe that's the best time to dig into it. If you homeschool, maybe you can implement it into your daily work. Find what works for you; there's no set of rules to follow!

*How long will it take us to complete the journal?*

That's the beauty of this journal experience—it will be different for everyone. There are enough activities within the journal for you and your child to fill up at least three months of time together, if you just do one activity each day or so (summer vacation, anyone?). But we recommend experimenting to find a pace that works best for you and your child.

*What's the best place to start?*

Right here is the best place to start! The Just for Us section is the bulk of the journal, and we recommend just starting on the first page and doing at least one of each of the four activity categories to give you an idea of what works for you. Be sure to take a look through the entire journal experience together so your child knows about the section especially for her and that there are great things to fill out throughout her section.

"Two people are better off than one,
for they can help each other succeed....
A person standing alone can be
attacked and defeated, but two can
stand back-to-back and conquer."

Ecclesiastes 4:9, 12 NLT

# Just for Us

Welcome to Just for Us! This part is all about you and your mom. There are four categories of things for you to do together:

TALK Together, Have FUN Together, Go DEEP Together, and CREATE Together.

You may pick one from any section at any time you like. You may even do one from each all in the same day! Make these pages—and your time together—your own, just for the two of you.

TALK Together: What is something that brings you joy?

Me:

_____

_____

_____

_____

_____

Mom:

_____

_____

_____

_____

_____

Tell me a Bible verse you love. What does this verse mean to you?

Me:

_____

_____

_____

_____

_____

Mom:

_____

_____

_____

_____

_____

What is your favorite season and why?

Me:

_____

_____

_____

_____

_____

Mom:

_____

_____

_____

_____

_____

What is something you thank Jesus for every day?

Me:

Mom:

What is your favorite memory? (This could be about a favorite gift,
favorite vacation time, favorite holiday, or just a favorite any kind of moment.)
Draw something that reminds you of that time.

*Me:*

Mom:

What is something you are afraid of?

Me:

_____

_____

_____

_____

_____

Mom:

_____

_____

_____

_____

_____

What is something that frustrates you, and what helps make you feel better?

Me:

_____

_____

_____

_____

_____

Mom:

_____

_____

_____

_____

_____

If you had $5, how would you spend it?

Me:

_____

_____

_____

_____

Mom:

_____

_____

_____

_____

What are your favorite games to play?

Me:

_____

_____

_____

_____

_____

Mom:

_____

_____

_____

_____

_____

TALK Together

What could your family do this week that would bless you?

*Me:*

_____

_____

_____

_____

_____

_____

_____

_____

_____

Mom:

Tell a story about a magical tree (and draw a picture) together!

What is something you've learned this year?

Me:

_____

_____

_____

_____

_____

_____

Mom:

_____

_____

_____

_____

_____

_____

What is your favorite part of the day?

Me:

_____

_____

_____

_____

_____

Mom:

_____

_____

_____

_____

_____

If you could be a superhero, what would your powers be?
(Write about it and draw a picture of your superhero costume!)

Me:

_____

_____

_____

_____

_____

*Mom:*

_____

_____

_____

_____

_____

Write a letter to someone you admire.

*Me:*

_____

_____

_____

_____

_____

_____

_____

_____

_____

_____

Mom:

_____

_____

_____

_____

_____

_____

_____

_____

_____

_____

What do you love most about weekends?

Me:

_____

_____

_____

_____

_____

Mom:

_____

_____

_____

_____

_____

Tell me about your favorite song.

Me:

_____

_____

_____

_____

_____

Mom:

_____

_____

_____

_____

_____

TALK Together

If you were to invent something, what would it be? (Write about it and draw a picture.)

Me:

_____

_____

_____

_____

_____

Mom:

_____

_____

_____

_____

_____

What is something you love about yourself? Why?

Me:

_____

_____

_____

_____

_____

Mom:

_____

_____

_____

_____

_____

What is something that makes you happy? Why?

Me:

_____

_____

_____

_____

_____

Mom:

_____

_____

_____

_____

_____

If you could be any animal, what would you be?
(Write about it and draw a picture of you as the animal.)

Me:

_____

_____

_____

_____

_____

Mom:

_____

_____

_____

_____

What would it be like if we lived underwater? Would you enjoy that?

Me:

_____

_____

_____

_____

_____

Mom:

_____

_____

_____

_____

_____

Tell me about something you've learned at church recently. How has that changed you?

Me:

_____

_____

_____

_____

_____

Mom:

_____

_____

_____

_____

_____

What does your PERFECT DAY look like? What would you do?

*Me:*

Mom:

_____

_____

_____

_____

_____

_____

_____

_____

_____

# Have Fun Together

"Our family is just one tent away from a full-blown circus."

# Tic-Tac-Toe

Have fun with a little friendly competition. One of you be X and one be O. Take turns placing your letters to see who can be first to get three of their letters in a row!

# Dots

The object of this game is to conquer more boxes than your opponent. Each person "moves" in turn by connecting 2 dots with a line. When you place the last "wall" of a single 4-dot square, you conquer the box. The player who conquers a box gets to put their first initial in the box and then go again. At the end, the player with the most boxes wins.

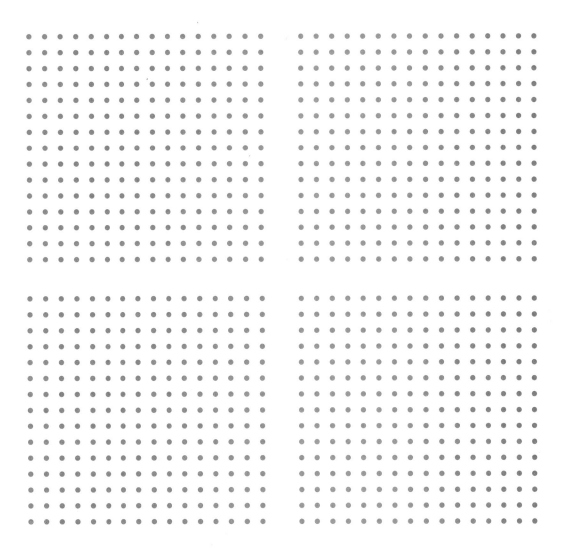

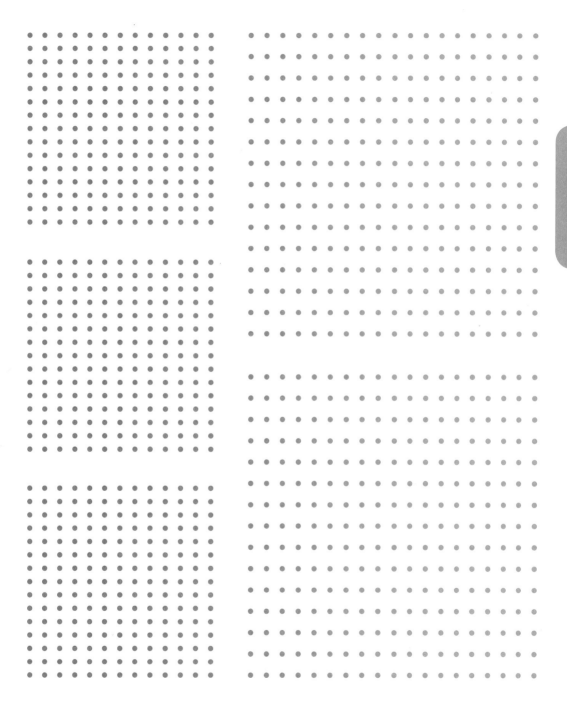

# Balloon Man

This is a spelling and guessing game.

The first player thinks of a word or short phrase (for example: sugar and spice) and draws a row of dashes—one dash for each letter of the answer (no proper nouns or slang). The other player guesses letters that might be in the word(s).

When the guess is correct, the first player writes in the right letter(s) in the answer. When the guess is incorrect, the first player draws a part of the balloon man (a picture of the whole balloon man character is shown).

The balloon man has 11 parts that can be drawn in this order: 1 body, 2 legs, 2 arms, 1 head, 2 eyes, 1 smile, 1 balloon string, 1 balloon. Keep track of the guessed letters on the side of the page.

The goal is to guess the answer before the balloon man is finished and flies away! Play as many times as you like (and get extra paper if you need it!).

Have FUN Together

## Word Search

See how fast you can find all the words in the word list! Look up, down, across, and diagonally.

Love, Family, Laugh, Together, Pray, Faith, Daughter, Son, Mother, Talk, Create, Fun

```
S W T S I C V B F T W K E B Y
T O O K R K M Y T R H G U A L
I J N E A T X J E B S T R V Z
X G A D A U G H T E R P I K E
D T P O K N T F O R M H O A Q
E C F E L E G U J F O G L H F
J F N A G P C N J I T A L K Q
W O L O M K G M W X H Z C S K
O I T K M I W U Z Z E D E P C
D K L C R L L U A F R B I E Q
Z B R V A Q I Y Y Q A Q T V F
K F H E Z J G A L E L Y P O I
N L E O B I D F W W W C I L J
Y N K R A P J G X Y I M B J R
W C B R Y T U T D A P P A O Q
```

# Would You Rather?

Take turns answering the questions below, and write some of your own! Would you rather ...

Be five years older or two years younger?

Be a master at drawing or an amazing singer?

Be a wizard or a superhero?

Fly or be invisible?

Be able to do backflips or break-dance?

Be able to only walk on all fours or only chirp like a bird?

Never be able to lie or never be able to cry?

Be able to see things really far away like a telescope or be able to see things up very close like a microscope?

Have lived 100 years ago or live 100 years in the future?

Meet your hero or win the lottery?

Live on an island in the middle of the ocean or at the top of a mountain?

Have everything in your house be the same color or every wall be a different color?

Be able to control fire or water?

Be able to remember everything you've ever heard or be able to perfectly imitate anyone's voice?

Eat the same meal for the rest of your life or only be able to drink smoothies?

Be able to change to any color or change your size at any time?

Never have homework again or be paid $20 for each homework assignment?

Have an elephant-sized cat or a cat-sized elephant?

Live in a hot-air balloon or a submarine?

Have super strength or super speed?

Stay a kid until you're 80 or instantly turn 40?

Always be kind or always be correct?

Meet Jesus in the past when He was on earth or meet Him where you live today?

Have FUN Together

# Picture Charades

You play this game like charades, except you draw clues instead of acting them out. Pick a category (movies, books, famous people, sayings, etc.). Then each of you write down some answers in that category on slips of paper and put them into a hat.

To start the game, the artist selects an answer from the hat and then tries to draw clues to get the other person to guess the right answer. Time the drawing to add to the fun—60 seconds for each turn. The winner is the one who guesses the most right answers or who draws the most ridiculous clues—you be the judge!

Ask your mom about the craziest thing she did as a kid.

Write the story here:

# Create your own scavenger hunt around your house!

List 10 clues for things players will have to find (for example: something blue, something Dad uses every morning, etc.).

1.

2.

3.

4.

5.

6.

7.

8.

9.

10.

Have FUN Together

## Celebrate creative holidays

Invent your own and make a list of them below. Then come back to this list and journal what you do to celebrate each one.

Have FUN Together

# Break the rules!

If you could stay up extra late for a special surprise, what would you like it to be? Ice-cream run? Late-night game night? Backyard movie? (Mom, take notes!)

## Write a silly song together!

It must include these 4 words (choose your favorite 4 words together):

1.

2.

3.

4.

# Teach each other your favorite dance moves!

Mom—show your child some of the moves from your childhood! Write the dance-move instructions below. Or take pics and print them out to keep them here.

Have FUN Together

## Who can blow the biggest bubble?

Get some bubble gum and see who can blow the biggest bubble. Track your bubbles. Measure them for added fun! Take pictures of your bubbles and compare them on your phone or computer, or if you can, print them out and glue them to this page.

# Baking contest!

Make some cupcakes and have a decorating contest. Allow siblings, Dad, or even the next-door neighbor to be the judge. Write down your results. (And draw an award ribbon for the winner!) If you'd like, you can take pictures of your cupcakes and glue them to this page.

Have FUN Together

# Blindfolded Banana Split

Put a blindfold on each other and create a banana split! The best banana split wins! (But really, you both win—because you get to eat it!)

Keep the blindfold on and each of you can attempt to draw a picture of your banana split on these pages.

Have FUN Together

# Who Am I?

You'll need sticky notes and a pen. Each of you should write down 3–5 characters (could be famous people, book or movie characters, or just people you know), with each character name on a separate sticky note. Hide your notes from each other. Then one at a time, put a sticky note on each other's forehead. The person with the note on the forehead has to ask the other person questions to guess who is named on the note.

When you are finished with the game, stick your notes here. Use one more note to write down 3–5 words that describe the other person: kids can describe their moms, and moms can describe their kids. Stick those notes here as well to make a sticky memory.

Have FUN Together

# Flashlight Tag!

Have some nighttime fun—let your child stay up a little late and enjoy a game of flashlight tag together. You simply have to "tag" the other person with the light of your flashlight. Invite siblings, Dad, or friends to join in!

When you're finished playing tag, have a coloring race! Pick a color and color in these two pages as fast as you can: you on one side and Mom on the other. The winner is the one who colors in his or her side faster. Ready, set, go!

Have FUN Together

# Go Deep Together

"And may you have the power to understand, as all God's people should, how wide, how long, how high, and how deep his love is."

Ephesians 3:18 NLT

#Goals

Write about the goals you have for this year here.

Me:

_____

_____

_____

_____

Mom:

_____

_____

_____

_____

Go DEEP Together

How Can I Pray for You?

*My prayer request:*

_____

_____

_____

_____

_____

*My prayer for Mom:*

_____

_____

_____

_____

_____

*Mom's prayer request:*

_____

_____

_____

_____

_____

*Mom's prayer for Me:*

_____

_____

_____

_____

_____

# What Does This Mean for Me?

Use these pages to read the Bible and find out what the verses mean together. Pick some verses you are curious about, or start with these suggestions:

Proverbs 3:5

Luke 6:31

John 3:16–21

Romans 3:23

Romans 8:1

Philippians 4:13

Colossians 3:2

Titus 3:5

Hebrews 13:8

## BIBLE VERSES:

Me: I think this is saying ...

_____

_____

_____

_____

_____

Mom: I think this is saying ...

_____

_____

_____

_____

_____

## What Does This Mean for Me?

### BIBLE VERSES:

*Me: I think this is saying ...*

_____

_____

_____

_____

_____

_____

_____

_____

_____

_____

Mom: I think this is saying ...

How Can I Pray for You?

*My prayer request:*

_____

_____

_____

_____

_____

*My prayer for Mom:*

_____

_____

_____

_____

_____

Mom's prayer request:

_____

_____

_____

_____

_____

Mom's prayer for Me:

_____

_____

_____

_____

_____

## What Does This Mean for Me?

BIBLE VERSES:

*Me: I think this is saying ...*

_____

_____

_____

_____

_____

_____

_____

Mom: I think this is saying ...

## What Does This Mean for Me?

### BIBLE VERSES:

*Me: I think this is saying ...*

_____

_____

_____

_____

_____

_____

_____

Mom: I think this is saying ...

_____

_____

_____

_____

_____

_____

_____

_____

_____

Go DEEP Together

How Can I Pray for You?

My prayer request:

_____

_____

_____

_____

_____

My prayer for Mom:

_____

_____

_____

_____

_____

Mom's prayer request:

_____

_____

_____

_____

_____

Mom's prayer for Me:

_____

_____

_____

_____

_____

## What Does This Mean for Me?

BIBLE VERSES:

*Me: I think this is saying ...*

Mom: I think this is saying ...

_____

_____

_____

_____

_____

_____

_____

_____

_____

_____

_____

Go DEEP Together

## What Does This Mean for Me?

## BIBLE VERSES:

*Me: I think this is saying ...*

_____

_____

_____

_____

_____

_____

_____

Mom: I think this is saying ...

How Can I Pray for You?

*My prayer request:*

_____

_____

_____

_____

_____

*My prayer for Mom:*

_____

_____

_____

_____

_____

Mom's prayer request:

_____

_____

_____

_____

_____

Go DEEP Together

Mom's prayer for Me:

_____

_____

_____

_____

_____

# Hard Questions

Here's a space to ask tough questions. Write your question below.
Then let your mom write an answer.

Sometimes I wonder ...

_____

_____

_____

_____

_____

_____

_____

_____

_____

_____

Here's Mom's answer:

## Hard Questions

Here's a space to ask tough questions. Write your question below.
Then let your mom write an answer.

Sometimes I wonder ...

_____

_____

_____

_____

_____

_____

_____

_____

_____

Here's Mom's answer:

Go DEEP Together

How Can I Pray for You?

*My prayer request:*

_____

_____

_____

_____

_____

*My prayer for Mom:*

_____

_____

_____

_____

_____

Mom's prayer request:

_____

_____

_____

_____

_____

Mom's prayer for Me:

_____

_____

_____

_____

_____

# Hard Questions

Here's a space to ask tough questions. Write your question below.
Then let your mom write an answer.

Sometimes I wonder ...

_____

_____

_____

_____

_____

_____

_____

_____

_____

Here's Mom's answer:

_____

_____

_____

_____

_____

_____

_____

_____

_____

_____

_____

Go DEEP Together

# Hard Questions

Here's a space to ask tough questions. Write your question below.
Then let your mom write an answer.

Sometimes I wonder ...

_____

_____

_____

_____

_____

_____

_____

_____

_____

Here's Mom's answer:

Go DEEP Together

How Can I Pray for You?

*My prayer request:*

_____

_____

_____

_____

_____

*My prayer for Mom:*

_____

_____

_____

_____

Mom's prayer request:

_____

_____

_____

_____

Mom's prayer for Me:

_____

_____

_____

_____

# Hard Questions

Here's a space to ask tough questions. Write your question below.
Then let your mom write an answer.

Sometimes I wonder ...

_____

_____

_____

_____

_____

_____

_____

_____

_____

Here's Mom's answer:

Go DEEP Together

# Hard Questions

Here's a space to ask tough questions. Write your question below.
Then let your mom write an answer.

Sometimes I wonder …

---

Here's Mom's answer:

_____

_____

_____

_____

_____

_____

_____

_____

_____

_____

Go DEEP Together

How Can I Pray for You?

*My prayer request:*

_____

_____

_____

_____

_____

*My prayer for Mom:*

_____

_____

_____

_____

_____

Mom's prayer request:

_____

_____

_____

_____

_____

Mom's prayer for Me:

_____

_____

_____

_____

_____

Go DEEP Together

# Create Together

"We didn't realise we were making memories,
we just knew we were having fun."

A. A. Milne, *Winnie-the-Pooh*

Start with the lines and dots on this page and make your own picture together. What will it become? A manatee-rhino-dragon? A tropical resort? A crowd of people? Draw and dream together. (For extra fun, don't tell each other what you are dreaming up, and see if the other person can guess where you are headed!)

CREATE Together

# Let's Make Chocolate Chip Cookies!

## FAMOUS* JAMES FAMILY CHOCOLATE CHIP COOKIES

*No actual awards have been received, but we think they are pretty amazing. ☺

**Ingredients:**
2 cups brown sugar
6 tbsp sugar
1 cup unsalted butter
2 eggs
4 tsp vanilla
3 1/2 cups flour
1 tsp baking soda
1 tsp baking powder
1 tsp salt
Chocolate chips or broken chocolate bar of your choice

Directions:
Cream butter and sugars in mixer until smooth. Add in eggs and vanilla.
Continue mixing.
Mix all dry ingredients in separate bowl.
Combine slowly into mixture until well blended.
Add in chocolate and mix.

Scoop onto baking sheet and bake at 375°F for 7 minutes.

# CELEBRATION CHOCOLATE CAKE

This cake is a crowd-pleaser in our house that we use for any and all celebrations!

**Ingredients:**
2 cups sugar
1 3/4 cups all-purpose flour
3/4 cup dark cocoa
1 1/2 tsp baking powder
1 1/2 tsp baking soda
1 tsp salt
2 eggs
1 cup milk
1/2 cup vegetable oil
2 tsp vanilla extract
1 cup boiling water

**Directions:**
Preheat oven to 350°F. Grease and flour two 9-inch round pans or one 13x9x2-inch baking pan.

Stir together sugar, flour, cocoa, baking powder, baking soda, and salt in large bowl. Add eggs, milk, oil, and vanilla; beat on medium speed of electric mixer 2 minutes. Stir in boiling water (batter will be thin). Pour batter into prepared pans.

Bake 30 to 35 minutes for round pans, 35 to 40 minutes for rectangular pan, or until wooden pick inserted in center comes out clean. Cool 10 minutes; remove from pans to wire racks. Cool completely.

# BUTTERCREAM FROSTING

**Ingredients:**
6 tbsp butter or margarine, softened
2 2/3 cups powdered sugar
1/2 cup dark cocoa
1/3 cup milk
1 tsp vanilla extract

**Directions:**
Beat butter in medium bowl. Add powdered sugar and cocoa alternately with milk, beating to spread consistency (additional milk may be needed). Stir in vanilla. Makes about 2 cups frosting.

CREATE Together

# EGG IN A HOLE

A favorite breakfast (or lunch or dinner!) and an easy first for kids to learn to cook!

**Ingredients:**
Bread
Butter
Egg
Salt and pepper

**Directions:**
Get your favorite cookie cutters and cut out the middle of the bread. You can also just use a biscuit cutter, the top of a glass, or anything you have in the kitchen to cut a hole in the bread. Preheat a skillet and butter each side of your bread while you wait for it to warm up. Place the bread in the skillet and crack an egg in the middle of the bread. Let the egg cook for a few minutes until it's ready to flip and then, using a spatula, turn it over in the skillet. Allow it to cook until it reaches your desired consistency. Season to your liking.

Enjoy!

# WAKE-UP CHOCO SMOOTHIE

Get-up-and-go smoothie! With mornings being hectic, sometimes a delicious, healthy smoothie is the answer to everyone's woes!

### Ingredients:
1 cup milk (your choice, we use almond milk)
1 banana
2 tbsp oats
1 tsp cocoa
1 tbsp peanut butter
Handful of ice cubes

### Directions:
Put all ingredients in your blender and blend until smooth. You can choose the amount of milk to add based on how you like the consistency of your smoothie. Double or triple (or on and on!) your recipe to serve everyone in your family!

CREATE Together

# BERRY-LICIOUS POPSICLE

Simple, beautiful, and packed with goodness! Perfect for an after-school treat, a summer snack by the pool, or just a side dish for any meal.

**Ingredients:**
2 cups fresh blueberries, raspberries, strawberries, and sliced bananas
2 cups plain greek yogurt
1/4 cup sugar

**Directions:**
Place everything in a blender and blend until either smooth or just a little chunky (this can be your preference). Fill popsicle cups or just small Dixie cups with mixture and place popsicle stick in the center. Freeze until solid.

Enjoy!

# FUN ON-THE-GO TACO BAR

This fun, creative meal is one the kids will be begging for! It works great for a fun family night outside, a gathering of friends, or if the kids have a bunch of friends over.

**Ingredients:**
1 lb hamburger meat
Taco seasonings
Taco fixings (cheese, sour cream, lettuce, tomato, salsa, queso—pick whatever your family loves!)
Single-serving-size bags of Doritos chips

**Directions:**
Prepare taco meat. Set out all your fixings in separate bowls. Use the Doritos bags as your bowls, and allow everyone to pile their taco fixings into their own bags!

CREATE Together

# HOW TO BUILD A LEMONADE STAND

Want to make a little extra money? Here are some ways to create your own lemonade stand to earn some money and have fun doing it!

**STEP ONE – Prepare!**
Choose a date and time. Plan ahead so you can market your stand. Your mom can help you post to social media to spread the word a day ahead of time so people can be prepared to stop by. Purchase all of your ingredients and supplies from the store: lemonade mix, cups, ingredients for cookies (try our famous chocolate chip cookie recipe in this book!), poster board, markers, or anything else you may need for your stand.

**STEP TWO – Make signs!**
You'll need a clearly marked sign with your pricing information. If your house isn't near a busy street, consider making a sign to put near the road to direct people your way!

**STEP THREE – Let's make lemonade!**
On the day of your stand, prepare your lemonade a few hours early and allow it to cool if you can. If you are also going to sell cookies or another treat, get those ready as well.

**STEP FOUR – Get set up!**
Make sure you set up before you are ready to open so you aren't rushing when customers are arriving. You'll need a table, a tablecloth if you have one (ask Mom if you can borrow an outdoor one if she has it), and something to hold all that money you're going to make. Bring your fresh lemonade out as soon as it's time to open up. It's always a good idea to have an ice chest with ice if it's an especially hot day.

**STEP FIVE – Have fun!**
Enjoy your time, get to know your neighbors, and make some new friends. Be sure to save some of that money you made, but go have some fun with it too!

# MAKE YOUR OWN PLAY CLAY

One of our favorite winter crafts is to make our own soft play clay. We always make a huge batch the day the kids get out of school for Christmas break and add peppermint extract to it, which makes the entire house smell AMAZING. But of course, this can be made anytime!

**Ingredients:**
3 cups flour
1 1/2 cups salt
6 tsp cream of tartar
3 cups water
3 tbsp oil
Food coloring until desired color
(1 oz of peppermint extract at the holidays)

**Directions:**
Combine ingredients in a saucepan and cook on stovetop over medium heat, constantly stirring. It will be ready once it starts to pull away from the pan and form a ball. Then you can move it to the counter and knead it until it feels like Play-Doh. Store in an airtight container when you're not playing with it.

CREATE Together

# HOMEMADE PUFFY SIDEWALK CHALK PAINT

Tired of the same old sidewalk chalk? Try out this fun, puffy sidewalk chalk paint that your kids can make, and enjoy decorating your driveway!

**Supplies needed:**
Squeeze bottles
Large mixing bowl
Rubber spatula

**Ingredients:**
1 cup flour
1 cup water
1 tbsp dish soap
Food coloring

**Directions:**
In your mixing bowl, combine water and flour until no lumps are seen. Stir in the dish soap until smooth. Next, add in the food coloring until you get your desired color. Pour your mixture into the squeeze bottle and you're ready to play! Use the sidewalk paint the same day; it doesn't keep well. Repeat process to make multiple colors in separate bottles.

To clean up—with a garden hose spray off the driveway immediately after the kids are done playing. If you leave it and let it dry, the food coloring can stain the driveway. If you want to leave it, substitute washable paint for the food coloring.

Practice your chalk pictures here!

# FRIENDSHIP ROCKS

A perfect way to show a friend how much you care.

**Supplies needed:**
A smooth, flat rock
Paint
Paintbrushes

**Directions:**
Have your child choose a friend to paint a friendship rock for. Your kid can put both of their names and a Bible verse on it, and decorate it anyway he or she likes. Once the rock dries, go hide the rock in the friend's yard and let the friend know he or she has a friendship rock to find! Use these pages to create some designs and practice drawing them for your rocks.

# MAKE YOUR OWN VOLCANO

Bring out the scientist in all of you and create this easy and fun mini volcano experiment right at home! I recommend doing this outside and you can easily wash away the mess with a water hose.

**Supplies needed:**
Plastic cup
Water
Baking soda
Dish soap
Washable paint
Vinegar

**Directions:**
Fill the plastic cup about 2/3 full of water. Add in 4 tbsp baking soda, 1 tsp dish soap, 1–2 oz of washable paint (depending on desired intensity of color). Give it a stir to mix everything together. Now add 1 cup of vinegar and watch the eruption!

## Fun tip

*If you use primary colors of paint, after the first explosion you can add another color, stir it in, and add more vinegar. You'll have a color-changing volcano!*

# CREATE A LASER MAZE

Rainy day? Too hot to play? Hate being stuck inside all day? No problem! We have the perfect activity that is sure to entertain everyone.

**Supplies needed:**
Yarn
A lot of yarn! (Check clearance racks at craft stores; it doesn't have to be anything special. Really, any kind of string will work.)

**Directions:**
Set the kids free to create a maze with the yarn, twisting it and tying it all through the house. Then they can create their own games to try to make their way through the maze. Don't forget to make a fun time of cleaning up also!

CREATE Together

## COLOR TOGETHER

Use the following pages to indulge your artistic leanings. Draw shapes of all sizes and color them in. Draw your house. Draw each other's faces. Draw what you'll look like in twenty years. Color stripes, circles, squares, or anything you like!

CREATE Together

## FREE SPACE

You are coming to the end of the Just for Us section. Take these couple pages to remember the best parts, dream up ideas for the future, pray for each other, or just draw more fun doodles together.

"Don't let anyone look down on you because you are young, but set an example for the believers in speech, in conduct, in love, in faith and in purity."

1 Timothy 4:12 NIV

# Just for Kids

STOP! Do not enter this section unless you have kid credentials, or unless you've been given permission by a qualifying young person.

Kids: use this space for praying, thinking, thanking, and remembering!

## PRAYING FOR THE FRUIT OF THE SPIRIT

The Holy Spirit gives us some really great gifts (and don't we all love getting gifts?). Those gifts are outlined in Galatians 5:22–23. These amazing qualities help us to be more like Jesus! We are going to spend some time looking at each fruit and praying to ask God to increase that quality in us so that we can be more like Him.

Get out your Bible and look up this scripture: Galatians 5:22–23. Write it out below:

# LOVE

Ask: How can I show love to someone around me?

Write out a prayer and ask God to help you show love.

# JOY

Ask: How can I show joy to someone around me?

Write out a prayer and ask God to help you show joy.

# PEACE

Ask: How can I show peace to someone around me?

Write out a prayer and ask God to help you show peace.

# PATIENCE

Ask: How can I show patience to someone around me?

Write out a prayer and ask God to help you show patience.

# KINDNESS

Ask: How can I show kindness to someone around me?

Write out a prayer and ask God to help you show kindness.

# GOODNESS

Ask: How can I show goodness to someone around me?

Write out a prayer and ask God to help you show goodness.

# GENTLENESS

Ask: How can I show gentleness to someone around me?

Write out a prayer and ask God to help you show gentleness.

# FAITHFULNESS

Ask: How can I show faithfulness to someone around me?

Write out a prayer and ask God to help you show faithfulness.

## SELF-CONTROL

Ask: How can I show self-control to someone around me?

Write out a prayer and ask God to help you show self-control.

## MY PRAYERS

Use the following pages to talk to God about whatever is on your mind. If you want to, share the prayers you write here with your mom so she can be praying for you too.

## MY PRAYERS

## MY PRAYERS

## MY PRAYERS

# MY PRAYERS

## MY PRAYERS

"Give all your worries and cares to God, for he cares about you."

1 Peter 5:7 NLT

# HELP ON HARD DAYS

How are you feeling?

I bet you have a lot of emotions, don't you? We all do! And there's nothing wrong with you. God made you exactly how He did on purpose and He's so proud of you—just like your mom is!

God gave us the Bible as a tool to help us when we are struggling. Did you have a hard day at school or can't stop fighting with your brother or sister? Maybe you're frustrated that something isn't quite going your way. You're not alone! Lots of people in the Bible had hard days and didn't get along with the people around them.

Read through the scriptures provided here, and then use the next several pages to journal and tell God all about how you are feeling and what's on your mind. He cares about you. He really does! Are you afraid? Tell Him. Are you angry? Tell Him.

Here are some verses to help you get started. Need more? Feel free to ask your mom how to find more scriptures to help with your exact feelings each day.

**When You're Feeling Afraid**
"When I am afraid,
I will trust in you.
In God, whose word I praise,
in God I trust; I will not be afraid.
What can mere mortals do to me?"
Psalm 56:3–4

**When You're Not Sure about Your Purpose**
"We know that all things work together for the good of those who love God, who are called according to his purpose."
Romans 8:28

**When You're Feeling Lost**
"Look, I am with you and will watch over you wherever you go."
Genesis 28:15

I'm feeling ...

Bible verses that help me:

I'm feeling ...

Bible verses that help me:

I'm feeling …

Bible verses that help me:

I'm feeling ...

Bible verses that help me:

I'm feeling ...

Bible verses that help me:

I'm feeling ...

Bible verses that help me:

I'm feeling ...

Bible verses that help me:

I'm feeling ...

Bible verses that help me:

I'm feeling ...

Bible verses that help me:

# GRATEFUL SPACE

Being grateful isn't always easy. Sometimes it takes practice. Use the next several pages to record things you are grateful for: good days, loving people in your life, happy surprises, and answers to prayer, among other things. Write down the date so you can remember when you were feeling grateful.

I am grateful for:                                                    Date:

_____

_____

_____

_____

_____

_____

_____

"Thanks be to God for his indescribable gift!"

2 Corinthians 9:15

I am grateful for:                                          Date:

_____

_____

_____

_____

_____

_____

_____

_____

_____

"And whatever you do, in word or in deed, do everything in the name
of the Lord Jesus, giving thanks to God the Father through him."

Colossians 3:17

I am grateful for:                                    Date:

_____

_____

_____

_____

_____

_____

_____

_____

"Give thanks to the LORD, for he is good.
His faithful love endures forever."

Psalm 136:1

I am grateful for:                                    Date:

_____

_____

_____

_____

_____

_____

_____

_____

_____

"Every good and perfect gift is from above, coming down from the
Father of lights, who does not change like shifting shadows."

James 1:17

I am grateful for:                                        Date:

_____

_____

_____

_____

_____

_____

_____

_____

"The Lord is my strength and my shield;
my heart trusts in him, and I am helped.
Therefore my heart celebrates,
and I give thanks to him with my song."

Psalm 28:7

I am grateful for:                                        Date:

_____

_____

_____

_____

_____

_____

_____

_____

_____

"Therefore, since we are receiving a kingdom that cannot be
shaken, let us be thankful. By it, we may serve God acceptably,
with reverence and awe, for our God is a consuming fire."

Hebrews 12:28–29

I am grateful for:                                          Date:

_____

_____

_____

_____

_____

_____

_____

_____

_____

_____

"I will give thanks to you, LORD, with all my heart;
I will tell of all your wonderful deeds."

Psalm 9:1 NIV

I am grateful for:                                    Date:

_____

_____

_____

_____

_____

_____

_____

_____

_____

"I give you thanks, O Lord, with all my heart....
As soon as I pray, you answer me;
you encourage me by giving me strength."

Psalm 138:1, 3 NLT

I am grateful for:                                        Date:

_____

_____

_____

_____

_____

_____

_____

_____

_____

"For everything created by God is good, and nothing is
to be rejected if it is received with thanksgiving."

1 Timothy 4:4

"Every time you cross my mind, I break out in exclamations of thanks to God."

Philippians 1:3 THE MESSAGE

## Memory Keeper

This is a place to write down things you never want to forget. The time you and your best friend built the best dirt-bike ramp. Or the time you befriended the new kid at school and how it made you feel. Write down a story about your family vacation and the crazy thing your little brother did that made you laugh so hard that milk came out of your nose.

Being a kid is fun, and you have so many fun things that fill your world. You do not want to forget the best things that happen!

Fill these pages with the things you never want to forget.

## Memory Keeper

## Memory Keeper

## Memory Keeper

## Memory Keeper

## Memory Keeper

## Memory Keeper

## Memory Keeper

## Memory Keeper

## Memory Keeper

# Just for Moms

"Jesus came to make all things new—including tired and weary moms."

# Dear Mama,

This space is for you. A place to reflect, pray, and praise God for this child He has given you. You'll find some short prompts here to help guide and point you back to Jesus. Some pages will have scriptures that you can study and pray through. Other days will have some guided points to pray specific things over your child.

Feel free to clip this section out and keep it private just for you. This will be a great keepsake and reminder of God's faithfulness through your parenting as you grow with your child in this season of life.

*Father, as I lean into being a more abundant mom, help me to press into You first and foremost. Show me the way to parent my child, and help me see this precious little one through Your eyes. Thank You for creating _____ the way that You did. I'm so grateful and honored to be _____ mother. Thank You for this journey; may You draw us all closer to You through it. Amen.*

## Pray for Wisdom

Pray that God would give your child the wisdom in making decisions and that they would learn to discern His voice against the noise of the world. Pray that your child would choose to obey the Lord and have a desire to follow Him and make wise choices.

"Now if any of you lacks wisdom, he should ask God—who gives to all generously and ungrudgingly—and it will be given to him."
James 1:5

"Do not be agitated by evildoers; do not envy those who do wrong.
For they wither quickly like grass and wilt like tender green plants.
Trust in the LORD and do what is good; dwell in the land and live securely.
Take delight in the LORD, and he will give you your heart's desires.
Commit your way to the LORD; trust in him, and he will act,
making your righteousness shine like the dawn, your justice like the noonday."
Psalm 37:1–6

"Trust in the LORD with all your heart, and do not rely on your own understanding;
in all your ways know him, and he will make your paths straight."
Proverbs 3:5–6

**Write your own prayer for your child:**

## Pray for Compassion

Pray for your child to have a kind and compassionate heart. Pray that their eyes would be opened to hurting people around them and they would be willing to step out of their comfort zone to extend a hand to help or be a friend in time of need. Pray that as they learn compassion, they would learn forgiveness and learn more about who Jesus is.

"And be kind and compassionate to one another, forgiving one another, just as God also forgave you in Christ."
Ephesians 4:32

"And walk in love, as Christ also loved us and gave himself for us, a sacrificial and fragrant offering to God."
Ephesians 5:2

"Therefore, as God's chosen ones, holy and dearly loved, put on compassion, kindness, humility, gentleness, and patience, bearing with one another and forgiving one another if anyone has a grievance against another. Just as the Lord has forgiven you, so you are also to forgive."
Colossians 3:12–13

**Write your own prayer for your child:**

# Pray for Friendships

Pray that God would surround your child with great friends now and throughout their lives. Pray for both godly friends who can lift them up and hold them accountable, as well as open doors for friendships in which they can be the light of Jesus. Pray for the friends in your child's life right now, that they would grow in godly character and be a good influence on your child's life.

"Two are better than one because they have a good reward for their efforts. For if either falls, his companion can lift him up; but pity the one who falls without another to lift him up."
Ecclesiastes 4:9–10

"Do not be deceived: 'Bad company corrupts good morals.'"
1 Corinthians 15:33

"Iron sharpens iron, and one person sharpens another."
Proverbs 27:17

**Write your own prayer for your child:**

## Pray for Leadership

Pray for leaders placed in your child's life. Pray that God would place wise and godly teachers, counselors, and friends who would be foundational in their growth as a person. Pray also that your child would grow into a wise leader for their generation and that God would equip them with the wisdom to make a difference.

"You are the light of the world. A city situated on a hill cannot be hidden. No one lights a lamp and puts it under a basket, but rather on a lampstand, and it gives light for all who are in the house. In the same way, let your light shine before others, so that they may see your good works and give glory to your Father in heaven."
Matthew 5:14–16

"Remember your leaders who have spoken God's word to you. As you carefully observe the outcome of their lives, imitate their faith."
Hebrews 13:7

"How happy is the one who does not walk in the advice of the wicked
or stand in the pathway with sinners or sit in the company of mockers!
Instead, his delight is in the LORD's instruction, and he meditates on it day and night.
He is like a tree planted beside flowing streams that bears its fruit in its season
and whose leaf does not wither. Whatever he does prospers."
Psalm 1:1–3

**Write your own prayer for your child:**

# Pray for Salvation

Pray that your child would come to know the Lord and, if they have already accepted Jesus as their Savior, that they would grow in a deep understanding of who He is. Pray that they would have the desire to follow Him each and every day of their life. Pray that your child would have a love and desire for the Word of God so they may grow up in the knowledge of what their salvation means.

"If you confess with your mouth, 'Jesus is Lord,' and believe in your heart that God raised him from the dead, you will be saved. One believes with the heart, resulting in righteousness, and one confesses with the mouth, resulting in salvation."
Romans 10:9–10

"For God loved the world in this way: He gave his one and only Son, so that everyone who believes in him will not perish but have eternal life."
John 3:16

"You will know the truth, and the truth will set you free."
John 8:32

**Write your own prayer for your child:**

## Pray for Health

Pray that God would keep your child's body strong, physically, emotionally, and spiritually and that they would be protected from disease, illness, and any other harm. Pray that He would equip them well and that they would be grateful for the use of a healthy mind and body. Pray for your child to be prepared to stand strong against anything that may come their way.

"My soul, bless the LORD, and all that is within me, bless his holy name.
My soul, bless the LORD, and do not forget all his benefits.
He forgives all your iniquity; he heals all your diseases.
He redeems your life from the Pit; he crowns you with faithful love and compassion.
He satisfies you with good things; your youth is renewed like the eagle."
Psalm 103:1–5

"But those who trust in the LORD will renew their strength;
they will soar on wings like eagles; they will run and not become weary,
they will walk and not faint."
Isaiah 40:31

"Therefore, since we also have such a large cloud of witnesses surrounding us, let us lay aside every hindrance and the sin that so easily ensnares us. Let us run with endurance the race that lies before us, keeping our eyes on Jesus, the source and perfecter of our faith. For the joy that lay before him, he endured the cross, despising the shame, and sat down at the right hand of the throne of God."
Hebrews 12:1–2

**Write your own prayer for your child:**

## Pray for Purity

Pray that God would help your child walk in purity and have a pure mind. Pray that He would protect their eyes, mouth, and heart. Pray that you would be able to answer questions clearly and help your child have an understanding of godly purity and guide them to focus on what is pure and true. Pray for their protection from things out of their control.

"How can a young man keep his way pure? By keeping your word."
Psalm 119:9

"Guard your heart above all else, for it is the source of life."
Proverbs 4:23

"Finally brothers and sisters, whatever is true, whatever is honorable, whatever is just, whatever is pure, whatever is lovely, whatever is commendable—if there is any moral excellence and if there is anything praiseworthy—dwell on these things."
Philippians 4:8

**Write your own prayer for your child:**

# Pray for Character

Pray that your child would be known by their character, always reflecting the heart of Jesus. Pray that you could be an example of what godly character is daily so they can grow in their values by following you and following Christ. Pray that they would have a desire to serve others and a heart for the Lord.

"Whatever you do, do it from the heart, as something done for the Lord and not for people."
Colossians 3:23

"For it is God who is working in you both to will and to work according to his good purpose."
Philippians 2:13

"Serve with a good attitude, as to the Lord and not to people."
Ephesians 6:7

**Write your own prayer for your child:**

# Pray for Honesty and Integrity

Pray that God would grow godliness deep in your child—that they would be more concerned about their character than their reputation. Pray that they would be a person who always strives for honesty and integrity in school, work, and relationships. Pray that they would bring honor to God in this specific area.

"May integrity and what is right watch over me, for I wait for you."
Psalm 25:21

"The one who lives with integrity lives securely,
but whoever perverts his ways will be found out."
Proverbs 10:9

"I pursue the way of your commands, for you broaden my understanding."
Psalm 119:32

**Write your own prayer for your child:**

## Pray to Dream Big and Have Big Joy!

Pray that God would place big dreams and big joy inside of your child. Pray that He would fulfill whatever His plan is for your child's life and that they would be an inspiration to everyone they come in contact with. Pray that they would live a life of passion, love, influence, and hope so that the world is impacted greatly by them.

"Jesus looked at them and said, 'With man this is impossible, but with God all things are possible.'"
Matthew 19:26

"Not that I have already reached the goal or am already perfect, but I make every effort to take hold of it because I also have been taken hold of by Christ Jesus. Brothers and sisters, I do not consider myself to have taken hold of it. But one thing I do: Forgetting what is behind and reaching forward to what is ahead, I pursue as my goal the prize promised by God's heavenly call in Christ Jesus."
Philippians 3:12–14

"Now to him who is able to do above and beyond all that we ask or think according to the power that works in us—to him be glory in the church and in Christ Jesus to all generations, forever and ever. Amen."
Ephesians 3:20–21

**Write your own prayer for your child:**

## Pray for You

Use this page to add a prayer for any specific concerns you have in mothering your child right now or any fears you have for the future. Remember that God gave this child to you—whether by birth, through adoption or fostering, or through marriage. He will equip you with everything you need to be the best mother you can be—just ask Him!

"Pursue a relationship with your kids based on the person God made each of them to be instead of what you think you should do as a mom."

Kara-Kae James, *Mom Up*

# GRATEFUL SPACE

Use the next several pages to practice the discipline of gratitude. Use these pages to record things you are grateful for: good days, loving people in your life, happy surprises, and answers to prayer, among other things. Write down the date so you can remember when you were feeling grateful.

*I am grateful for:*                                      *Date:*

_____

_____

_____

_____

_____

_____

_____

"Thanks be to God for his indescribable gift!"

2 Corinthians 9:15

*I am grateful for:*                                               *Date:*

_____

_____

_____

_____

_____

_____

_____

_____

_____

_____

"And whatever you do, in word or in deed, do everything in the name
of the Lord Jesus, giving thanks to God the Father through him."

Colossians 3:17

*I am grateful for:*                    *Date:*

_____

_____

_____

_____

_____

_____

_____

_____

_____

_____

_____

"Give thanks to the LORD, for he is good.
His faithful love endures forever."

Psalm 136:1

I am grateful for:                                        Date:

_____

_____

_____

_____

_____

_____

_____

_____

_____

"Every good and perfect gift is from above, coming down from the
Father of lights, who does not change like shifting shadows."

James 1:17

I am grateful for:                                    Date:

_____

_____

_____

_____

_____

_____

_____

_____

_____

"The LORD is my strength and my shield;
my heart trusts in him, and I am helped.
Therefore my heart celebrates,
and I give thanks to him with my song."

Psalm 28:7

*I am grateful for:*                                    *Date:*

_____

_____

_____

_____

_____

_____

_____

_____

_____

_____

_____

"Therefore, since we are receiving a kingdom that cannot be
shaken, let us be thankful. By it, we may serve God acceptably,
with reverence and awe, for our God is a consuming fire."

Hebrews 12:28–29

I am grateful for:                                    Date:

_____

_____

_____

_____

_____

_____

_____

_____

_____

_____

"I will give thanks to you, LORD, with all my heart;
I will tell of all your wonderful deeds."

Psalm 9:1 NIV

I am grateful for:                                    Date:

_____

_____

_____

_____

_____

_____

_____

_____

_____

_____

"I give you thanks, O LORD, with all my heart....
As soon as I pray, you answer me;
you encourage me by giving me strength."

Psalm 138:1, 3 NLT

*I am grateful for:*                    *Date:*

_____

_____

_____

_____

_____

_____

_____

_____

_____

_____

"For everything created by God is good, and nothing is
to be rejected if it is received with thanksgiving."

1 Timothy 4:4

"God wants something so sweet for us in motherhood, to thrive in the chaos and live freely in this calling."

Kara-Kae James, *Mom Up*

# Memory Keeper

Let these pages be a safe space to remember funny things your child said or did. A place to write down a story of that family vacation you never want to forget.

The years slip by so fast, and those little moments are the things we want to cling to. Those are the things that bring us unfathomable joy. The way your child's hand fits so perfectly into yours. The way they outgrew you in fourth grade (how did that happen so quickly?). The way they wink at you when they get out of the car to head into school each morning.

Cherish those moments and remember each one of them. Fill these pages with the things you never want to forget.

"The best things about memories is making them."

## Memory Keeper

## Memory Keeper

## Memory Keeper

## Memory Keeper

## Memory Keeper

_____

_____

_____

_____

_____

_____

_____

_____

_____

_____

## Memory Keeper

# Memory Keeper

# Memory Keeper

## FREE SPACE

You are coming to the end of the Just for Moms section, and the end of this journal. Take these couple pages to remember the best parts, dream up ideas for the future, pray for your child again, or lay your head down and take a nap!

# FREE SPACE

"It is easier to build strong children than to repair broken men."

# WHERE TO GO FROM HERE

You made it! Well done! We hope and pray that you have grown so much as individuals and together. Use these last pages to think about your next steps.

What is something you learned about your mom through doing this journal that you never knew before?

_____

_____

_____

_____

What is something you learned about your child through doing this journal that you never knew before?

_____

_____

_____

_____

## Now What?

It's easy to keep talking when you have a tool that helps you, but what now? You don't want to lose this amazing connection you've created. Make a list of some ways you can continue to keep the lines of communication fun and open between each other:

Mom's ideas:

_____

_____

_____

_____

My ideas:

_____

_____

_____

_____

Write a note in the space provided to express how grateful you are for each other.

Dear Mom,

_____

_____

_____

_____

_____

_____

_____

_____

_____

_____

_____

Dear _____,

_____

_____

_____

_____

_____

_____

_____

_____

_____

_____

_____

What I love about my mom:

_____

_____

_____

_____

_____

What I love about my child:

_____

_____

_____

_____

_____

# About the Authors—US!

Write an author bio for each other. Use the questions that follow to help you get started. And if you'd like, stick a photo of the two of you to one of these pages.

About Mom:

About the Kid:

How old are you?

What's your favorite food?

Best book you read this year?

Favorite thing to do in your free time?

Favorite subject in school?

Do you have a nickname?

What are you learning about right now that you enjoy?

Something you've always wanted to do?

Have you ever written any other books or poems? If so, what?

## A Challenge and a Prayer

### CHALLENGE

It would be really easy to close the pages of this book, stick it on a shelf, and return to your usual routine. But I have a challenge for you. Don't allow the mundane of everyday life get the better of you. Don't slip into the daily rhythm and forget this precious time together and what you've built here. It's too important. It's too meaningful. As you prepare to transition into the next phase of life, walking into the preteen and teen years and beyond, keep your communication strong. Be there for each other. Have the hard conversations with grace, and be open to listen and learn. You will both be better for it as you grow together. Keep Jesus at the center of your relationship, and always pray for each other. You are doing a great job, and it's going to be a wild and fun ride! Enjoy it!

### PRAYER

*Father, thank You for the gift of this time together. Thank You for the fun, the laughter, and the ways we've grown closer to You. Keep our hearts connected through the years, and always guide us back to each other for a safe space to lean on. God, protect our home and our family. Let us continue to seek You first so that Your Spirit overflows into everything we do. Thank You for the gift we have in each other. Amen.*

# About Kara-Kae

Kara-Kae James is a writer and encourager passionate about seeing women's lives changed and impacted through the gospel. She is the founder and executive director of Thrive Moms, a ministry dedicated to seeing moms step out of survival mode and into the thriving, abundant life that God calls them to. She is also the author of the book *Mom Up: Thriving with Grace in the Chaos of Motherhood* and the Thrive Moms Bible studies *Abundance*, *Freedom*, and *Rest*.

Kara-Kae is married to her husband, Brook, and is mom to three girls and the world's most energetic little boy. She is passionate about pouring into moms because she knows firsthand that many moms are struggling and in desperate need of a reminder that God loves us and we are doing His holy work.

## What Is Thrive Moms?

Thrive Moms is a ministry for moms to encourage and inspire you to do more than JUST SURVIVE motherhood. We believe God wants us to thrive and walk confidently in who He calls us to be as mothers.

We are a ministry seeking to serve, inspire, and empower imperfect moms with the perfect grace of Christ. We strive to accomplish this through our collaborative blog, daily online encouragement, Bible studies, local community resources, and more!

Learn more about Thrive Moms at thrivemoms.com.

MORE BOOKS FROM KARA-KAE AND THRIVE MOMS

*Mom Up: Thriving with Grace in the Chaos of Motherhood*

**Thrive Moms Bible Studies:**

*Abundance: Discovering a Full Life in Christ*

*Freedom: Letting Go and Embracing Christ*

*Rest: Finding Stillness in the Midst of Busy*

# ᄁM

## EMPOWERING IMPERFECT MOMS WITH GOD'S PERFECT GRACE.

We invite you to join the Thrive Moms' Community—
a community of real women who are stepping out of
survival mode and into thriving, abundant life with Christ.
We focus on community, intentionality as moms,
finding our rest in the Lord, and embracing the
wonderfully chaotic moments of everyday life.
We continue to push each other deeper into God's Word
and know that we are better when we stand together.

### JOIN US AT THRIVEMOMS.COM

@thrivemoms

Elise Aileen Photography

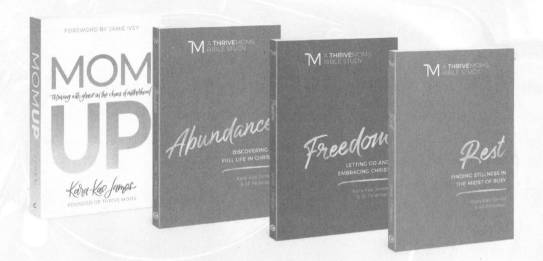